Flower Farms
Julie Haydon

Chapter 1	**Flowers**	2
Chapter 2	**Flower Farms**	4
Chapter 3	**Fields and Greenhouses**	6
Chapter 4	**Growing Flowers**	8
Chapter 5	**Caring for Flowers**	12
Chapter 6	**Harvesting the Flowers**	14
Chapter 7	**Transporting the Flowers**	17
Chapter 8	**The Uses of Flowers**	18
Chapter 9	**Multiple Choice**	22
Glossary and Index		24

Chapter 1: Flowers

I like flowers.
Sometimes I buy flowers from a flower shop.

The **florist** told me that the flowers in the shop come from a flower farm. I want to learn more about flower farms.

Flower Farms

What is a flower farm?

A flower farm is a place where flowers are grown for sale.

Some flower farms grow one kind of flower.
Some flower farms grow
many different kinds of flowers.

Chapter 3 Fields and Greenhouses

Where do the flowers on a flower farm grow?

Some flowers are grown in fields.
Some flowers are grown in special buildings called **greenhouses**.

a greenhouse

Why do flower growers use greenhouses?

Greenhouses protect the flowers from bad weather. Flower growers can choose how much heat, light, and water to give the flowers in a greenhouse.

Chapter 4 Growing Flowers

Do flowers on flower farms grow from seeds?

Flower growers can grow flowers from seeds, but some flowers are grown from bulbs or cuttings. Some flowers are grown by grafting.

A bulb is an underground bud.

Cuttings are parts of plants that are cut from other plants and planted in the ground. New plants grow from cuttings.

Grafting is when part of one plant is joined to another plant.
The two parts grow into each other and make a new plant.

Chapter 5: Caring for Flowers

How do flower growers care for their flowers?

Plants are living things.
Flower growers must make sure that their plants get enough sun, plant food, and water to stay healthy.

Flower growers must keep the soil clean and free of weeds. They must keep the plants safe from insects and **diseases**.

This machine is spraying liquid over the flowers. This helps to keep them safe from insects and diseases.

Harvesting the Flowers

How do flower growers pick the flowers on a flower farm?

Most flowers on a flower farm are picked, or **harvested**, by hand.

What happens to the harvested flowers?

The harvested flowers are sorted and put into bunches.

How do flower growers keep their flowers fresh?

The bunches of flowers are put into buckets of water.
Then they are stored in a cool room.
This helps to keep the flowers fresh.

Transporting the Flowers

Where are the flowers sent?

The flowers are put onto trucks.
The trucks take the flowers to shops,
markets, and factories.
Some flowers are even sent to other countries.

Chapter 8 The Uses of Flowers

What are the flowers used for?

Some flowers are sold to people to put in their homes.
Some flowers are dried and sold as **decorations**.

dried flowers

fresh flowers

Some flowers are used to make perfumes, soaps, oils, and even some food and drinks.

tea made from flowers

oil made from flowers

Many people give flowers as gifts or use flowers in **celebrations**.

birthday

wedding

thank you

Valentine's Day

Mother's Day

Chapter 9: Multiple Choice

1. A florist sells:
   - flour
   - flowers
   - food

2. Special buildings that protect flowers from bad weather are:
   - bluehouses
   - redhouses
   - greenhouses

3. Animals are living things, and so are:
   - plants
   - machines
   - rocks

4. People who grow flowers on farms are:
   - dairy farmers
   - flower growers
   - ranchers

Glossary

celebrations	special events
decorations	things that are nice to look at
diseases	sicknesses
florist	a person who sells flowers
greenhouses	special buildings where plants are grown
harvested	picked when ready

Index

bulbs 8, 9
cuttings 8, 10
fields 6
florist 3, 22
flower growers 3, 7, 8, 12–14, 16, 23
gifts 20
grafting 11
greenhouses 6–7, 22
seeds 8

Multiple Choice answers: 1. flowers, 2. greenhouses, 3. plants, 4. flower growers